The Online Entrepreneur's Handbook

Making Your First $100 Online

AMOKE EMMANUEL

DEDICATION

This book is dedicated to my readers especially those who this book will impact values to their life.

CONTENTS

ACKNOWLEDGMENTS

I thank the Almighty God who gave me the inspiration to write this book and also thank my family and the Simple Sale community for their support. I also thank Augusta Ezeani for her own support in the course of the research for the book.

She is the CEO of Austy Pastries, the bakery produces snacks, you can contact me if you need her products.

INTRODUCTION

Welcome to "The Online Entrepreneur's Handbook: Unlocking the Digital Wealth Frontier." In this comprehensive guide, we embark on a journey into the vast realm of online entrepreneurship, where opportunities to thrive and succeed abound.

The digital age has opened up unprecedented possibilities for aspiring entrepreneurs to establish their ventures and reach a global audience. The internet offers an ecosystem where innovation, creativity, and resourcefulness can flourish, and barriers to entry are lower than ever before. Whether you're an experienced business owner seeking to expand your reach or a budding entrepreneur ready to take your first step, this handbook will equip you with the knowledge and strategies you need to thrive in the digital landscape.

Our journey begins with Chapter 1, where we delve into the foundations of the digital landscape. Understanding the evolution of the internet and its impact on businesses is crucial to making informed decisions as an online entrepreneur. We'll explore the technological advancements that have shaped the digital world, the rise of e-commerce, and the opportunities it presents for growth and prosperity.

In subsequent chapters, we'll address critical aspects of online entrepreneurship, from building and enhancing your online presence to formulating a winning business strategy that aligns with your goals. We'll unlock the potential of digital marketing, guiding you through the intricacies of social media, SEO, and effective content creation. Additionally, we'll investigate the power of e-mail marketing, affiliate marketing, and the concept of drop shipping as valuable income streams for your online business.

As we navigate through the vast digital landscape, we'll also explore the world of online advertising, understanding its dynamics and learning how to leverage it effectively. Moreover, we'll dive into the realm of e-learning and digital product creation, uncovering how these innovative ventures can drive revenue and expand your influence.

Data analytics play a pivotal role in the digital realm, and we'll emphasize the importance of leveraging data to make informed decisions, enhance customer experiences, and optimize business processes. Finally, we'll address the crucial aspect of securing your digital empire, safeguarding your online presence, and protecting your customers' data and trust.

Throughout this handbook, we'll combine theoretical knowledge with practical advice, real-world case studies, and actionable insights from successful online entrepreneurs. Each chapter aims to equip you with valuable tools, empowering you to navigate the digital wealth frontier confidently.

So, whether you're a seasoned business owner seeking to transition to the digital landscape or an enthusiastic individual ready to embrace the world of online entrepreneurship, "The Online Entrepreneur's Handbook: Unlocking the Digital Wealth Frontier" is your definitive guide to building a thriving and prosperous online venture.

THE DIGITAL LANDSCAPE

We'll explore the inception and growth of the internet, tracing its transformation from a mere communication tool to a global platform that has revolutionized the way we live, work, and do business.

The Internet Revolution:

The digital age began with the birth of the internet, a groundbreaking invention that connected the world like never before. We'll delve into the origins of the internet, the pioneers behind its creation, and how it rapidly expanded across the globe.

E-Commerce: A Paradigm Shift in Business:

One of the most significant outcomes of the digital revolution is e-commerce. We'll uncover the roots of online shopping, its initial challenges, and how it became an integral part of the modern economy. Understanding the principles of e-commerce will lay the groundwork for your online entrepreneurial journey.

Seizing Opportunities in the Digital Era:

The internet has democratized entrepreneurship, allowing individuals from all walks of life to establish online businesses. In this section, we'll explore the vast array of opportunities available in the digital space and how you can tap into them to unleash your entrepreneurial potential.

Overcoming Digital Challenges:

With great opportunities come unique challenges. We'll address common obstacles faced by online entrepreneurs, such as competition, cybersecurity threats, and maintaining credibility in the digital realm. Equipped with this knowledge, you'll be better prepared to tackle hurdles head-on.

Embracing a Digital Mindset:

To thrive in the digital landscape, a shift in mindset is essential. We'll discuss the characteristics of successful online entrepreneurs, the importance of adaptability, and how embracing a digital mindset can fuel your growth and success.

Navigating the Future of Digital Entrepreneurship:

The digital landscape is constantly evolving, and keeping up with emerging trends is crucial. We'll conclude this chapter by peering into the future of online entrepreneurship, identifying potential game-changers, and discussing how you can position yourself for sustained success.

With Chapter 1 as our starting point, we're ready to embark on an exciting journey through the digital wealth frontier. As you dive into the subsequent chapters, remember that knowledge combined with action is the key to unlocking your online entrepreneurial dreams. Let's begin our adventure!

NAVIGATING E-COMMERCE

Before venturing into the realm of online selling, it's crucial to grasp the multifaceted e-commerce ecosystem. We'll explore the different types of e-commerce models, such as B2B (Business-to-Business), B2C (Business-to-Consumer), C2C (Consumer-to-Consumer), and more. Understanding these models will help you identify the most suitable approach for your online business.

Selecting Your Niche:

A critical aspect of e-commerce success lies in identifying and narrowing down your niche. We'll guide you through the process of conducting market research, analyzing trends, and recognizing gaps in the market. By honing in on a specific niche, you can target your audience effectively and establish a distinct brand identity.

Building Your Online Store:

The foundation of a successful e-commerce venture is a well-designed online store. We'll discuss the various e-commerce platforms available, each with its own set of features and benefits. From user-friendly platforms for beginners to robust solutions for established businesses, you'll learn to choose the one that aligns with your needs and vision.

Design and User Experience (UX):

Aesthetics and user experience are vital for retaining customers and encouraging repeat business. In this section, we'll explore the principles of effective website design and how to create a seamless, intuitive shopping experience. Learn how to optimize your website for different devices to accommodate the preferences of modern consumers.

Payment Gateways and Security:

Securing online transactions is paramount to building trust with your customers. We'll dive into the world of payment gateways, encryption protocols, and best practices for maintaining a secure e-commerce environment. Gain insights into fraud prevention measures and compliance with data protection regulations.

Fulfillment and Shipping:

Efficient order fulfillment and shipping are essential components of a successful e-commerce business. We'll discuss various fulfillment options, such as in-house fulfillment, third-party logistics (3PL) providers, and drop shipping. Discover strategies to streamline your shipping process, manage inventory effectively, and deliver exceptional customer service.

Pricing and Promotions:

Crafting an effective pricing strategy can significantly impact your sales and profitability. We'll explore dynamic pricing, discount strategies, and the psychology behind pricing decisions. Additionally, we'll discuss promotional tactics, including flash sales, limited-time offers, and loyalty programs, to attract and retain customers.

Customer Service and Support:

In the digital world, exceptional customer service sets you apart from the competition. Learn how to build a customer-centric approach, handle inquiries and complaints promptly, and foster long-term customer relationships. Happy customers are more likely to become brand advocates, driving organic growth for your business.

Analyzing E-Commerce Performance:

Data-driven decision-making is a hallmark of successful e-commerce entrepreneurs. We'll delve into the key performance indicators (KPIs) you should monitor, such as conversion rate, average order value (AOV), and customer lifetime value (CLV). Armed with this knowledge, you can identify areas for improvement and optimize your e-commerce operations.

Expanding Your E-Commerce Empire:

As your e-commerce venture grows, expansion opportunities may arise. We'll explore options such as expanding to new markets, diversifying product offerings, and utilizing cross-border e-commerce. Learn how to scale your business while maintaining the same level of quality and customer satisfaction.

Sustainability in E-Commerce:

With increasing environmental awareness, sustainability has become a crucial consideration for businesses. We'll discuss sustainable e-commerce practices, from eco-friendly packaging to reducing carbon footprints. Embracing sustainability not only benefits the planet but also resonates with environmentally conscious consumers.

As you immerse yourself in Chapter 2, you'll gain valuable insights into the world of e-commerce, equipping yourself with the knowledge and tools to establish a thriving online store. Remember, success in e-commerce requires continuous learning, adaptation, and a passion for providing value to your customers. Stay committed to your vision, and let's pave the way to e-commerce excellence together.

BUILDING YOUR ONLINE PRESENCE

Establishing your brand and making meaningful connections with your target audience will set the stage for long-term success.

Crafting Your Brand Identity:

Your brand is more than just a logo; it's the essence of your business. We'll delve into the process of crafting a compelling brand identity that reflects your values, mission, and unique selling proposition. Discover how to resonate with your audience emotionally and create a brand that leaves a lasting impression.

Building a Professional Website:

A professional website is the cornerstone of your online presence. We'll dive deeper into the elements of an effective website, from engaging content and intuitive navigation to visually appealing design. Learn the importance of responsive web design to ensure your website looks great on all devices.

Harnessing the Power of Blogging:

Blogging is a powerful tool for establishing authority and driving organic traffic to your website. We'll explore the art of creating valuable and shareable blog content that addresses your audience's pain points and interests. Through consistent blogging, you can position yourself as an industry thought leader and build a loyal readership.

The Influence of Social Media:

Social media platforms offer unprecedented opportunities to connect with your target audience on a personal level. We'll discuss popular platforms like Facebook, Instagram, Twitter, LinkedIn, and YouTube, and how to leverage them effectively. Learn to create engaging content, interact with followers, and use analytics to refine your social media strategy.

Video Content Marketing:

Video content is a dominant force in the digital landscape. We'll explore the benefits of video marketing, from building trust and conveying complex ideas to increasing user engagement. Discover how to create compelling video content that aligns with your brand and resonates with your audience.

Podcasting for Thought Leadership:

Podcasting has emerged as a powerful medium to share knowledge and connect with audiences worldwide. We'll delve into the world of podcasting, from planning and recording to promoting and monetizing your podcast. Learn how to establish yourself as a thought leader in your niche through this intimate and engaging medium.

Email Marketing Strategies:

Email marketing remains a cornerstone of successful online businesses. We'll discuss strategies for building and nurturing an email list, crafting persuasive email campaigns, and optimizing your email marketing funnel.

Discover how to personalize your messages and deliver value to your subscribers.

Leveraging Influencer Marketing:

Influencer marketing has transformed the way businesses reach their audiences. We'll explore how to identify suitable influencers in your niche, forge authentic partnerships, and measure the effectiveness of your influencer campaigns. Learn to harness the power of influencer endorsements to expand your brand reach.

Online Forums and Communities:

Participating in online forums and communities can be a valuable way to connect with potential customers and industry peers. We'll guide you through the do's and don'ts of forum engagement, establishing yourself as a valuable contributor, and leveraging these platforms to boost your online presence.

The Impact of Customer Reviews:

Customer reviews have a profound influence on consumer behavior. We'll discuss the significance of managing online reviews, responding to feedback, and encouraging positive reviews from satisfied customers. Embrace the power of social proof to build credibility and trust in your brand.

Monitoring Your Online Reputation:

In the digital age, your online reputation can make or break your business. We'll explore tools and techniques to monitor and manage your online reputation effectively. Responding proactively to feedback and addressing potential crises will safeguard your brand's reputation.

Engaging with Webinars and Live Events:

Webinars and live events provide excellent opportunities to engage with your audience in real-time. We'll discuss how to plan and execute successful webinars, as well as the benefits of hosting or participating in live events. These interactions foster meaningful connections and enhance your brand's visibility.

The Power of Partnerships:

Collaborating with complementary businesses can yield mutually beneficial results. We'll explore partnership opportunities, such as co-marketing initiatives and joint ventures, and how these alliances can accelerate your growth and expand your reach.

Measuring Online Presence Success:

Throughout your online presence-building journey, measuring success is essential. We'll delve into key metrics and analytics tools to track your progress, gauge the effectiveness of your efforts, and make data-driven decisions for continuous improvement.

Also Remember that building your online presence is an ongoing process. Embrace creativity, authenticity, and consistency in your approach. By mastering the art of connecting with your audience, you'll forge strong bonds that lead to lasting customer relationships and sustainable business growth.

CRAFTING A WINNING BUSINESS STRATEGY

A well-defined strategy serves as a roadmap, guiding your decisions and actions to achieve your business objectives effectively.

Setting Clear Goals and Objectives:

The first step in crafting a winning business strategy is to set clear and achievable goals. We'll explore the process of defining your short-term and long-term objectives, ensuring they align with your overall vision. Well-defined goals provide direction and motivation for your entrepreneurial journey.

Identifying Target Markets and Customer Segments:

Understanding your target markets and customer segments is vital for tailoring your offerings and marketing efforts. We'll delve into market research techniques to identify your ideal customers, their needs, and pain points. Armed with this knowledge, you can create products and services that resonate with your audience.

Competitive Analysis and Differentiation:

A thorough competitive analysis helps you identify your strengths and weaknesses relative to your competitors. We'll guide you through the process of differentiating your business, offering unique value propositions, and positioning your brand effectively in the market.

Value Chain and Business Model:

Analyzing your value chain and business model is essential to identify opportunities for efficiency and profitability. We'll explore various business models, from subscription-based to freemium, and discuss how to optimize your value chain to deliver exceptional value to your customers.

SWOT Analysis for Informed Decision-Making:

Conducting a SWOT (Strengths, Weaknesses, Opportunities, Threats) analysis provides valuable insights for strategic decision-making. We'll discuss how to capitalize on your strengths, address weaknesses, seize opportunities, and mitigate potential threats to your business.

The Power of Innovation:

Innovation is a key driver of success in the digital era. We'll explore strategies to foster a culture of innovation within your organization, encourage creativity, and continually refine your offerings to meet evolving market demands.

Financial Planning and Budgeting:

A robust financial plan is critical for the sustainability of your business. We'll discuss the essentials of financial planning, including revenue projections, expense management, and budget allocation for marketing and growth initiatives.

Creating a Marketing Strategy:

An effective marketing strategy is essential for attracting and retaining customers. We'll delve into various digital marketing channels, from search engine marketing (SEM) to social media advertising. Learn how to create cohesive campaigns that engage your audience and drive conversions.

The Importance of Customer Retention:

Customer retention is just as crucial as customer acquisition. We'll explore tactics to foster customer loyalty, such as loyalty programs, personalized communication, and excellent post-purchase support. Loyal customers become brand advocates, helping to expand your customer base through word-of-mouth.

Scalability and Growth:

As your business grows, scalability becomes a key consideration. We'll discuss strategies for scaling your operations, maintaining product quality, and preserving a positive customer experience as you handle increased demand.

Crisis Management and Risk Mitigation:

In the dynamic digital landscape, crises and risks are inevitable. We'll explore proactive approaches to crisis management, including contingency planning and reputation management. Be prepared to navigate challenges with resilience and a strategic outlook.

Evaluating and Adjusting Your Strategy:

A winning business strategy requires continuous evaluation and refinement. We'll discuss how to assess the effectiveness of your strategy, gather feedback from stakeholders, and make data-driven adjustments to stay on the path to success.

Embracing Corporate Social Responsibility (CSR):

As an online entrepreneur, embracing corporate social responsibility can have a profound impact on your business and the community. We'll explore ways to integrate CSR initiatives into your business model, fostering a positive brand image and contributing to social and environmental causes.

Empowering Your Team:

A successful business strategy requires a motivated and empowered team. We'll discuss leadership principles, team building, and strategies for fostering a positive work environment. Invest in your team's growth and well-being to drive collective success.

Balancing Innovation and Stability:

In the ever-changing digital landscape, striking a balance between innovation and stability is crucial. We'll explore how to foster a culture of innovation while maintaining core stability to ensure your business stays relevant and adaptable.

THE POWER OF DIGITAL MARKETING

We'll begin by delving into the various digital marketing channels at your disposal. From Search Engine Optimization (SEO) and Pay-Per-Click (PPC) advertising to content marketing and email marketing, each channel offers unique opportunities to connect with your audience. Gain insights into the strengths and nuances of each platform to craft an integrated marketing strategy.

Crafting Compelling Content for Digital Audiences:

Content is the heart of digital marketing. We'll discuss the art of crafting compelling and valuable content that resonates with your target audience. Whether it's blog posts, videos, infographics, or podcasts, learn how to captivate your audience and establish your brand as an authoritative voice in your industry.

The Role of SEO in Visibility and Traffic:

Search Engine Optimization (SEO) is critical for driving organic traffic to your website. We'll delve into SEO best practices, keyword research, on-page optimization, and link-building strategies. Implementing effective SEO techniques will help your website rank higher in search engine results, increasing visibility and driving qualified traffic.

Unleashing the Power of PPC Advertising:

Pay-Per-Click (PPC) advertising enables you to reach potential customers through targeted ads. We'll explore popular PPC platforms like Google Ads and social media advertising. Learn how to set up and optimize PPC campaigns, ensuring your advertising budget is maximized for results.

Social Media Marketing Strategies:

Social media has revolutionized how businesses engage with their audience. We'll discuss social media marketing strategies, including content planning, community management, and leveraging social media analytics. Harness the power of social media to foster brand loyalty and drive conversions.

Email Marketing for Relationship Building:

Email marketing remains one of the most effective channels for nurturing customer relationships. We'll explore email marketing automation, segmentation, and personalized messaging. Create engaging email campaigns that deliver value to your subscribers and keep them informed about your products and promotions.

Harnessing the Potential of Influencer Marketing:

Influencers can amplify your brand's reach and credibility. We'll delve into influencer marketing strategies, from identifying the right influencers to structuring partnerships. Discover how to leverage influencers to create authentic connections with your target audience.

The Art of Affiliate Marketing:

Affiliate marketing is a performance-based marketing strategy that can drive significant revenue for your business. We'll discuss affiliate program management, commission structures, and nurturing relationships with affiliates. Learn how to build a network of affiliates who promote your products passionately.

Leveraging Data and Analytics:

Data is the foundation of successful digital marketing campaigns. We'll explore web analytics tools and data-driven decision-making. Learn to interpret data insights to optimize your marketing efforts and enhance customer experiences.

Embracing Personalization and User Experience:

Personalization is a key driver of customer satisfaction and loyalty. We'll discuss the value of personalized marketing messages, product recommendations, and user experiences. Enhance your customers' journey by tailoring your offerings to their preferences and needs.

The Power of Viral Marketing and User-Generated Content:

Viral marketing and user-generated content can catapult your brand to new heights. We'll explore strategies to encourage user-generated content and create viral marketing campaigns. Engage your audience in sharing your brand message and expanding your reach organically.

Navigating Online Advertising Trends:

Digital marketing trends evolve rapidly. We'll explore emerging trends such as augmented reality (AR) marketing, interactive content, and voice search optimization. Stay ahead of the curve by embracing innovative marketing approaches.

Ethical Considerations in Digital Marketing:

As a responsible digital entrepreneur, ethical marketing practices are paramount. We'll discuss transparency, data privacy, and promoting inclusivity in your marketing campaigns. Uphold ethical standards to build trust with your audience and foster a positive brand reputation.

Evaluating Digital Marketing ROI:

Measuring the return on investment (ROI) of your digital marketing efforts is essential. We'll discuss key performance indicators (KPIs) and analytics tools to track the effectiveness of your campaigns. Make data-driven decisions to allocate resources strategically.

Remember that digital marketing is an ever-evolving landscape. Stay informed about the latest trends and technologies, and be open to experimenting with new strategies. With a solid understanding of digital marketing, you can drive brand visibility, engage your audience, and achieve your business goals in the vast digital wealth frontier.

SOCIAL MEDIA MASTERY

Mastering social media is essential for establishing your online presence and growing your digital empire.

Choosing the Right Social Media Platforms:

Not all social media platforms are created equal, and each caters to different demographics and content types. We'll discuss the most popular platforms, such as Facebook, Instagram, Twitter, LinkedIn, Pinterest, and TikTok. Understand the unique strengths of each platform and select the ones that align with your target audience and brand objectives.

Crafting a Cohesive Social Media Strategy:

A well-defined social media strategy is the backbone of successful social media marketing. We'll explore the components of a cohesive strategy, including content planning, posting schedules, and community engagement. A strategic approach ensures your social media efforts contribute to your overall business goals.

Engaging Content Creation:

Content is king on social media. We'll delve into the art of creating engaging content that resonates with your audience. From eye-catching visuals to compelling captions and hashtags, discover how to craft content that drives likes, comments, shares, and ultimately, conversions.

Building a Follower Base and Community:

Building a loyal follower base is a gradual process. We'll discuss organic growth strategies, such as creating shareable content, hosting social media contests, and collaborating with influencers. Learn how to foster a sense of community around your brand and encourage user-generated content.

The Power of Social Media Advertising:

Social media advertising enables precise targeting and amplification of your message. We'll explore the intricacies of running effective social media ad campaigns, from setting campaign objectives to creating captivating ad creatives. Maximize your advertising budget to reach potential customers effectively.

Influencer Collaboration and Partnerships:

Influencer marketing extends beyond mere advertising. We'll discuss how to build genuine relationships with influencers, fostering authentic partnerships that resonate with their followers. Embrace influencers as brand ambassadors who embody your values and beliefs.

Leveraging Social Media Analytics:

Data-driven decision-making is vital for social media success. We'll explore social media analytics tools that provide valuable insights into audience behavior, content performance, and campaign effectiveness. Use analytics to refine your strategies and optimize your social media efforts.

Engaging with Your Audience:

Social media is a two-way street, and engaging with your audience is essential. We'll discuss best practices for responding to comments, messages, and mentions promptly. Cultivate meaningful interactions to build trust and loyalty among your followers.

Managing Social Media Crisis:

In times of crisis, social media can become a powerful tool to communicate effectively with your audience. We'll explore crisis management strategies, including transparency, empathy, and swift response. Handle crises with professionalism and maintain a positive brand image.

Social Media Listening and Market Research:

Social media platforms offer a treasure trove of consumer insights. We'll delve into social media listening and market research techniques to understand customer preferences, pain points, and sentiment. Use this knowledge to refine your offerings and marketing messages.

Harnessing Social Media Trends:

Social media trends change rapidly. We'll discuss how to spot and leverage emerging trends, such as new content formats, challenges, and viral movements. Embrace trends creatively to capture your audience's attention and stay relevant in the social media landscape.

Advocacy and Social Impact:

Social media provides an opportunity to advocate for social causes and drive positive change. We'll explore how to use your platform to raise awareness, support charitable initiatives, and align your brand with meaningful social impact.

Social Media Etiquette and Brand Voice:

Maintaining a consistent brand voice and adhering to social media etiquette are vital. We'll discuss guidelines for posting, handling criticism, and addressing controversial topics. A thoughtful and respectful approach will strengthen your brand's reputation.

Tracking Social Media ROI:

Measuring the return on investment (ROI) of your social media efforts is crucial for resource allocation. We'll explore social media KPIs and tools to track performance metrics. Analyze data to understand the impact of social media on your business's bottom line.

As you practice Chapter 6, remember that social media mastery requires dedication, creativity, and a genuine commitment to engaging with your audience. Embrace the ever-changing social media landscape, experiment with new approaches, and continuously refine your strategies to unlock the full potential of this powerful digital marketing tool.

Search Engine Optimization (SEO) Unveiled

Understanding SEO is essential for establishing a strong online presence and attracting potential customers to your digital empire.

The Importance of SEO in the Digital Landscape:

Search Engine Optimization (SEO) is the process of optimizing your website and content to rank higher in search engine results. We'll explore the significance of SEO in driving organic traffic, building credibility, and gaining a competitive edge in the digital marketplace.

The Search Engine Ecosystem:

To master SEO, you need to understand the workings of search engines. We'll discuss the key players, such as Google, Bing, and Yahoo, and explore their algorithms and ranking factors. Stay updated on search engine updates and algorithm changes that can impact your website's visibility.

Keyword Research and Analysis:

Keyword research is the foundation of effective SEO. We'll guide you through the process of identifying relevant keywords and understanding search intent. Learn how to prioritize keywords that align with your business goals and have high search volume and low competition.

On-Page SEO Optimization:

On-page SEO involves optimizing individual web pages to improve their search engine rankings. We'll explore techniques such as optimizing meta tags, headings, and content structure. Implement on-page SEO best practices to enhance your website's visibility to search engines and users.

Creating High-Quality and Engaging Content:

Content is central to successful SEO. We'll discuss the importance of high-quality, valuable, and engaging content that addresses the needs of your target audience. Learn how to use keywords naturally in your content and create content that earns backlinks and social shares.

The Power of Backlinks and Link Building:

Backlinks are crucial for building authority and trust with search engines. We'll explore link building strategies, including outreach, guest posting, and content marketing. Earn high-quality backlinks from reputable sources to boost your website's credibility.

Technical SEO and Website Performance:

Technical SEO involves optimizing the technical aspects of your website for search engines. We'll discuss website speed, mobile responsiveness, site structure, and URL optimization. A technically sound website ensures smooth crawling and indexing by search engines.

Local SEO for Geo-Targeted Visibility:

If you have a local business, local SEO is essential for driving foot traffic and local customers to your store. We'll explore techniques such as Google My Business optimization, local citations, and customer reviews. Harness the power of local SEO to dominate the search results in your area.

User Experience (UX) and SEO:

A positive user experience is critical for both SEO and customer satisfaction. We'll discuss UX principles such as site navigation, readability, and mobile-friendliness. Enhance user experience to reduce bounce rates and improve search engine rankings.

Measuring and Analyzing SEO Success:

SEO is an ongoing process, and measuring its success is essential. We'll explore SEO metrics and analytics tools to track your website's performance. Monitor organic traffic, keyword rankings, and conversion rates to assess the effectiveness of your SEO efforts.

Staying White-Hat: Ethical SEO Practices:

Ethical SEO practices are essential for sustainable growth. We'll discuss white-hat SEO techniques and ethical guidelines set by search engines. Avoid black-hat SEO practices that can result in penalties and reputational damage.

International SEO and Multilingual Optimization:

If you target international audiences, international SEO and multilingual optimization are crucial. We'll explore hreflang tags, geotargeting, and content localization. Ensure your website is accessible and relevant to global audiences.

The Future of SEO:

SEO is continuously evolving. We'll explore emerging trends, such as voice search, artificial intelligence, and video SEO. Stay ahead of the curve by adapting your SEO strategies to upcoming innovations.

Integrating SEO with Other Digital Marketing Channels:

SEO does not exist in isolation. We'll discuss how to integrate SEO with other digital marketing channels, such as social media, content marketing, and email marketing. A cohesive approach maximizes the impact of your marketing efforts.

SEO for E-Commerce and Online Marketplaces:

For e-commerce entrepreneurs, SEO is vital for driving product visibility and sales. We'll explore SEO strategies for product pages, category pages, and online marketplaces. Optimize your e-commerce platform to attract potential customers and boost conversions.

THE ART OF EFFECTIVE EMAIL MARKETING

We explore the art of effective email marketing—an indispensable strategy for nurturing customer relationships, driving conversions, and maximizing the lifetime value of your audience. Mastering email marketing is crucial for building a loyal customer base and achieving sustainable business growth.

Understanding the Power of Email Marketing:

Email marketing remains one of the most potent and cost-effective marketing channels. We'll discuss the advantages of email marketing, such as direct communication with your audience, personalized messaging, and the ability to track and measure campaign performance.

Building a High-Quality Email List:

Your email list is the foundation of successful email marketing. We'll explore techniques for building a high-quality and engaged email subscriber base. From opt-in incentives to landing page optimization, learn how to attract and retain subscribers who genuinely value your content.

The Importance of Segmentation and Personalization:

Personalization is key to effective email marketing. We'll discuss the significance of segmenting your email list based on demographics, behavior, and interests. Tailor your email content to deliver personalized and relevant messages that resonate with each segment.

Crafting Compelling Email Content:

The content of your emails determines their effectiveness. We'll delve into the art of crafting compelling email content, including attention-grabbing subject lines, engaging copy, and clear calls-to-action. Learn to strike a balance between promotional content and valuable information.

Designing Responsive and Visually Appealing Emails:

Email design plays a crucial role in capturing your audience's attention. We'll explore responsive design principles to ensure your emails look great on all devices. Discover how to use visuals, brand elements, and whitespace effectively to create visually appealing emails.

Automating Email Campaigns:

Automation streamlines your email marketing efforts and improves efficiency. We'll discuss automated email campaigns, such as welcome sequences, abandoned cart reminders, and re-engagement campaigns. Implement automation to deliver timely and relevant messages to your subscribers.

Nurturing Customer Relationships:

Email marketing is a powerful tool for nurturing customer relationships. We'll explore strategies for maintaining regular communication, addressing customer inquiries, and providing exceptional customer support. Cultivate a strong bond with your audience to foster brand loyalty.

Leveraging Email for Sales and Conversions:

Email is a prime channel for driving sales and conversions. We'll discuss sales-focused email campaigns, such as product launches, flash sales, and exclusive offers. Optimize your email marketing funnel to guide subscribers toward making a purchase.

A/B Testing and Optimization:

Continuous improvement is essential for email marketing success. We'll explore A/B testing techniques to test different elements of your emails, such as subject lines, calls-to-action, and visuals. Use data-driven insights to optimize your email campaigns for better results.

Email Deliverability and Spam Compliance:

Ensuring your emails reach the inbox is crucial. We'll discuss best practices for improving email deliverability, including sender reputation management, list hygiene, and spam compliance. Stay compliant with email regulations to maintain a positive sender reputation.

Analyzing Email Marketing Performance:

Measuring the performance of your email campaigns is vital for refinement and growth. We'll explore email marketing metrics, such as open rates, click-through rates (CTR), and conversion rates. Analyze data to gauge the success of your campaigns and identify areas for improvement.

Integrating Email Marketing with Other Channels:

Email marketing is most effective when integrated with other digital marketing channels. We'll discuss how to align your email marketing efforts with social media, content marketing, and website optimization. Create a cohesive marketing ecosystem that reinforces your brand message.

Email Marketing for E-Commerce:

For e-commerce entrepreneurs, email marketing is a powerful tool for driving repeat purchases and customer retention. We'll explore e-commerce email strategies, such as product recommendations, cart abandonment emails, and post-purchase follow-ups.

Navigating Email Marketing Trends:

The email marketing landscape is continually evolving. We'll explore emerging trends, such as interactive emails, AI-driven personalization, and dynamic content. Embrace innovative email marketing trends to stay ahead of the competition.

Ethical Considerations in Email Marketing:

Responsible and ethical email marketing practices are essential for building trust with your subscribers. We'll discuss the importance of permission-based marketing, transparent communication, and GDPR compliance. Respect your subscribers' privacy and preferences.

MAXIMIZING CONVERSION WITH LANDING PAGES

Mastering the art of crafting high-converting landing pages can significantly impact your online success.

Understanding the Purpose of Landing Pages:

Landing pages serve a specific purpose: to guide visitors toward taking a desired action. We'll discuss the different types of landing pages, including lead generation pages, sales pages, and event registration pages. Understanding their roles will help you create targeted and effective landing experiences.

Designing Landing Pages for Conversions:

A well-designed landing page can make all the difference in converting visitors into customers. We'll explore the elements of high-converting landing pages, including compelling headlines, persuasive copy, clear calls-to-action, and visually appealing layouts. Create a seamless user experience that encourages action.

Crafting Irresistible Value Propositions:

Your value proposition is the heart of your landing page. We'll discuss the importance of a clear and compelling value proposition that communicates the unique benefits of your offer. Craft messages that resonate with your target audience and address their pain points.

Optimizing Landing Page Forms:

Forms are a critical component of lead generation landing pages. We'll explore form optimization strategies to strike the right balance between collecting valuable information and minimizing friction for visitors. Reduce form abandonment and increase form completion rates.

The Role of Visuals and Media:

Visual elements can enhance the impact of your landing pages. We'll discuss the use of images, videos, and multimedia content to convey your message effectively. Visuals can evoke emotions, establish credibility, and showcase your products or services.

Mobile-Friendly Landing Pages:

Mobile responsiveness is crucial for landing page success. With the majority of users accessing the internet on mobile devices, we'll explore techniques to ensure your landing pages look and function flawlessly on smartphones and tablets.

Building Trust and Credibility:

Trust is essential for driving conversions. We'll discuss how to build credibility through testimonials, customer reviews, trust badges, and security seals. Establishing trust will ease customer hesitations and increase their confidence in your offer.

Implementing Urgency and Scarcity:

Creating a sense of urgency and scarcity can spur action on your landing pages. We'll explore tactics such as limited-time offers, countdown timers, and inventory scarcity to motivate visitors to take immediate action.

A/B Testing for Landing Page Optimization:

A/B testing is crucial for refining your landing pages. We'll discuss how to conduct A/B tests to compare different elements and variations. Test headlines, calls-to-action, colors, and layouts to uncover the most effective combinations.

Analyzing Landing Page Performance:

Data-driven decision-making is essential for landing page success. We'll explore landing page metrics and analytics tools to track performance. Monitor conversion rates, bounce rates, and user behavior to identify areas for improvement.

Integrating Landing Pages into Campaigns:

Landing pages are integral to various marketing campaigns. We'll discuss how to integrate landing pages with email marketing, social media, and PPC advertising. Create cohesive campaigns that lead visitors from awareness to conversion.

Landing Page SEO Best Practices:

Optimizing landing pages for search engines is vital for organic traffic. We'll explore landing page SEO techniques, including keyword optimization, meta tags, and URL structure. Attract relevant organic traffic to your landing pages.

Cross-Selling and Upselling on Landing Pages:

Landing pages present opportunities for cross-selling and upselling. We'll discuss how to strategically offer complementary products or upgrades to enhance the customer experience and increase revenue.

Customizing Landing Pages for Segments:

Segmenting your audience allows you to create personalized landing page experiences. We'll explore dynamic content and personalization techniques to deliver tailored messages that resonate with each segment.

The Role of Emotional Appeal:

Emotional appeal can be a potent tool on landing pages. We'll discuss how to evoke emotions that align with your brand and message. Emotional connections can significantly influence purchase decisions.

The Future of Landing Pages:

Landing page trends continue to evolve. We'll explore emerging trends, such as interactive landing pages, AI-driven personalization, and voice search optimization. Stay ahead of the curve by adapting your landing pages to future innovations.

Ethical Considerations in Landing Page Design:

Ethical landing page practices build trust with your audience. We'll discuss transparency, honest communication, and avoiding deceptive tactics. Uphold ethical standards to establish long-term customer relationships.

BUILDING A THRIVING ONLINE COMMUNITY

Creating a supportive community can be a game-changer for your business in the digital landscape.

Understanding the Importance of Online Communities:

Online communities provide a space for your audience to connect, share experiences, and feel a sense of belonging. We'll discuss the benefits of building an online community, such as increased brand loyalty, valuable feedback, and word-of-mouth marketing.

Defining Your Community's Purpose and Values:

A strong community is built on a clear purpose and shared values. We'll explore how to define your community's mission and establish guidelines for member conduct. A well-defined purpose fosters a cohesive and engaged community.

Selecting the Right Platform for Your Community:

Choosing the right platform is crucial for the success of your online community. We'll discuss various options, such as forums, social media groups, and dedicated community platforms. Select the platform that aligns with your community's needs and preferences.

Fostering Community Engagement:

Active engagement is the lifeblood of a thriving community. We'll explore strategies to encourage discussions, facilitate interactions, and spark conversations among community members. Engaged members will contribute to the vibrancy of your community.

Cultivating a Positive Community Culture:

Creating a positive and inclusive community culture is paramount. We'll discuss the role of community managers in setting the tone, addressing conflicts, and nurturing a welcoming environment. A positive culture promotes constructive dialogue and mutual respect.

Providing Value to Community Members:

Your community must offer value to its members. We'll explore ways to provide educational resources, exclusive content, and member benefits. Demonstrating value strengthens members' commitment to the community.

Leveraging User-Generated Content (UGC):

User-generated content is a powerful asset for your community. We'll discuss how to encourage and showcase UGC, such as testimonials, product reviews, and member-generated discussions. UGC fosters authenticity and social proof.

Hosting Community Events and Activities:

Community events and activities foster a sense of unity and excitement. We'll explore virtual meetups, webinars, AMAs (Ask Me Anything), and challenges. Host events that align with your community's interests and goals.

Rewarding and Recognizing Community Contributions:

Recognizing and rewarding active members incentivize participation. We'll discuss gamification, badges, and rewards for community engagement. Acknowledge members' contributions to foster a culture of appreciation.

Harnessing Feedback for Improvement:

Community feedback is a valuable source of insights. We'll explore methods to collect feedback, such as surveys and polls. Use feedback to improve your products, services, and community experience.

Collaborating with Influencers and Thought Leaders:

Influencers and thought leaders can add value to your community. We'll discuss collaborations, guest appearances, and Q&A sessions with industry experts. Influencers' participation can attract new members and elevate your community's status.

Scaling Your Community as You Grow:

As your community expands, scalability becomes essential. We'll discuss strategies for managing a growing community, such as adding moderators, creating subgroups, and implementing automation. Ensure your community remains cohesive and supportive.

Monitoring Community Health and Performance:

Monitoring community metrics helps assess its health and performance. We'll explore key community metrics, such as engagement rates, retention, and churn. Data-driven insights guide your community management decisions.

Integrating Your Community with Brand Strategy:

Your community is an extension of your brand. We'll discuss how to align your community with your overall brand strategy and messaging. A cohesive brand presence strengthens community identity.

Ethical Considerations in Community Management:

Ethical community management builds trust with members. We'll discuss privacy, data protection, and transparency. Uphold ethical practices to ensure a safe and respectful community space.

The Future of Online Communities:

Online communities continue to evolve. We'll explore emerging trends, such as virtual reality communities, niche-focused groups, and AI-powered community platforms. Embrace innovation to stay at the forefront of community building.

ABOUT THE AUTHOR

Hi, I am Amoke Emmanuel, a programmer and an author who coaches people on the different ways to make money online. You can read more about me on Simple Sale, https://simplesale.com.ng where I provide amazing tips on how to be in good relationship with your pet.